BO BARKS

The First Pooch Tells All!

DEDICATION

To Debra Woodward, who made all this
possible, a thousand barks of thanks!

And to Revi, and all dogs everywhere, who
give such joy to their human companions.

Photo Credits: Cover image, Back Cover image: © The White House/Getty Images; Interiors: © The White House/Getty Images; © The White House/Getty Images; © Larry Downing/Reuters/Corbis; © Mandel Ngan/Getty Images; © Michael Reynolds/epa/Corbis; © Mandel Ngan/Getty Images; © The White House/Getty Images; © The White House/Getty Images; © George Skadding/Getty Images; © Bettmann/Corbis; © Bob Gomel/Getty Images; © Corbis; © Bettmann/Corbis; © Reuters/Corbis; © Reuters/Corbis; © Jennifer Young/Getty Images; © Luke Frazza/Getty Images; © Yuri Gripas/Getty Images; © Mandel Ngan; © Brendan Smialowski/Getty Images; © Larry Downing/Reuters/Corbis; © Mandel Ngan/Getty Images; © Saul Loeb/Getty Images; © Lucas Dolega/epa/Corbis; © Saul Loeb/Getty Images; © Adrian Dennis/Getty Images; © Grant V. Faint/Getty Images; © The White House/Getty Images; © Hiroshi Higuchi/Getty Images; © Larry Downing/Reuters/Corbis; © Grant Faint/Getty Images; © Larry Downing/Reuters/Corbis; © Charles Ommanney/Getty Images; © Alex Wong/Getty Images; © Saul Loeb/Getty Images; © Larry Downing/Reuters/Corbis; © Charles Ommanney/Getty Images; © The White House/Getty Images; © Joe Drivas/Getty Images; The White House/Getty Images; © Mark Wilson/Getty Images; © The White House/Getty Images; © The White House/Getty Images.

10 9 8 7 6 5 4 3 2 1

Printed and bound in China.

First Dad Barack said it best—"Bo's got star quality."

POTUS: President of the United States

FLOTUS: First Lady of the United States

FIDOTUS: First Dog of the United States

TWITTER: Micro-blogging service that allows you to keep friends and strangers updated on your every activity — no matter how mundane or sleep-inducing. The act of sending these updates is known as tweeting.

MALIA and SASHA: My big sisters

PAPARAZZI: Photographers without borders (my new BFF)

BFF: Best Friends Forever

State of the Union: A yummy speech that POTUS was supposed to present to the nation.

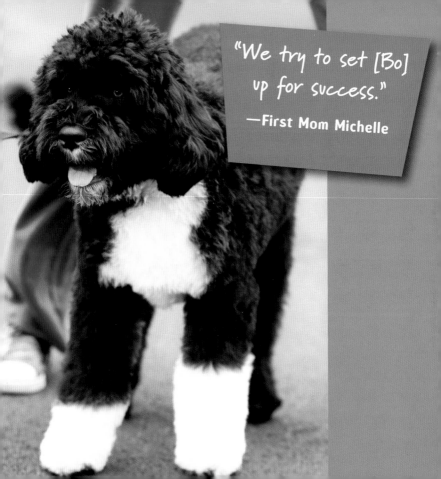

"We try to set [Bo] up for success."

—First Mom Michelle

First Dog Bo's Secret Service Dossier

SUBJECT: FIDOTUS Bo Obama

CODE NAME: Manolo

MEDIA NICKNAME: Commander-in-Leash

REASON: Addicted to shoes (eating them, that is)

BREED: Portuguese Water Dog (PWD)

VIP CONNECTION: The First Family

FAVORITE HANGOUTS: Rose Garden, press room with paparazzi, First Lady's closet

ROMANTIC AFFILIATIONS: TBTD (too busy to date)

FAVORITE DRINK: Tap water, straight up

FAVORITE SPORT: 300-yard dash

FAVORITE MOVIES: *Dog Day Afternoon*, *101 Dalmatians*, *Best in Show*, *The Truth About Cats and Dogs*

SUSPECTED ENEMIES: Rush Limbaugh, Ann Coulter, Glenn Beck, Sarah Palin's family dog

CLASSIFIED Unauthorized Viewing Strictly Forbidden

Everybody Deserves a Second Chance in Life...

Things didn't work out with the family who first adopted me — and gave me the name Charlie. Maybe they were worried that I refused to respond to that name. How could I? I always knew I was "Bo" and destined for greatness. After they returned me to my breeder, I admit I was a little depressed. I binged on doggie biscuits and stopped playing with my Tug-a-Rope and squeaky toys. Most days, I could be found sprawled on my doggy pillow, watching reruns of Lassie and Scooby-Doo (that's when I knew I had hit rock bottom). Then the call came from Senator Kennedy and his wife, who wanted to take a meeting with me . . . and things began looking up. They were the proud companions of Cappy, one of my nine sibs, and they enrolled me in puppy finishing school to get me ready for the new home where I was meant to be. One day, a big limo pulled up to take me to 1600 Pennsylvania Avenue. And the rest, as they say, is history.

They had me at "Hello."

First Lady Michelle tries out positive reinforcement training to get me to roll over on command.

Gimme the ball...

Here I am, chasing quarterback Big BO.

The agony of defeat...
Getting tackled on the 10-yard line with a minute to go!

FROM BO'S WHITE HOUSE SCRAPBOOK OF FAMOUS FIRST PETS

It was rumored that President Franklin Delano Roosevelt had asked First Dog Fala to become his vice president in the tumultuous election of 1944. Fala declined and Truman got the post. Here's a rare photo of FDR and my role model Fala taking a joyride around D.C.

He went thataway! Top Dog Charlie loved to lead President Kennedy and the Secret Service on wild squirrel chases.

Here's President Nixon
with Checkers, the dog who
saved his political career.
Now that's what I call
a "rescue dog"!

Former Dog-in-Chief
Liberty dictating his
memoirs to President Ford.
Oh, for a book deal!

Amy Carter with Grits, her spaniel mix,
a present from her fifth grade teacher.
Apparently, Grits's tenure in the
White House was brief. He annoyed
Amy's Siamese cat and when he bit a
guest and left his calling card on the
Lincoln Room carpet, Grits was
dispatched back to Amy's teacher.
Fame is so fleeting...

It's a "ruff" life. President George H. W. Bush's dog, Millie, stretching out in the Oval Office after an exhausting day of decision-making.

First Pooch Millie stepping off Air Force One after returning from Camp Canine. Now that's what I call an entrance!

Rumor has it that President Clinton's cat, Socks, was smarter than she looked. But here she is incriminating herself at a White House Press Conference. Does she look like a deer caught in the headlights or what?

Here's President Clinton's canine pal, Buddy, capturing Socks's favorite ball and making a run for it. That was a day that will live in White House history. As President Clinton said, "I did better with the Palestinians and the Israelis... than I've done with Socks and Buddy."

Suppose they gave a press conference and nobody came?

Here's President George W. Bush's dog, Barney, being stood up by the media at his final press conference. You gotta feel sorry for the guy.

FROM THE DESK OF BELTWAY BO

Dear Snoopy,

I appreciate your taking time out from your battles with the Red Baron (and that equally ferocious force of nature, Lucy) to write me. However, I don't think it was very gracious or sportsmanlike of you to ask me to abdicate my position as First Dog, just because now I'm getting more publicity than you. Good grief! It's true, for years you were the reigning champ, but it's time to make room for the new kid on the block. Just to show I don't hold any grudges, I hope you and C.B. and the gang will come visit me in the White House — I promise to even let you sleep on the roof.

Your humble chum,

Bo

STATE OF THE UNION SPEECH GOES BELLY UP!

Insiders say First Dog Bo is to blame

It was an embarrassing case of "my dog ate my homework" for President Obama yesterday. Except this time the excuse was all too real. The drama unfolded last night as millions of viewers tuned in to watch the 44th President's highly anticipated State of the Union address. First, the teleprompters malfunctioned. Then, a clearly exasperated President Obama admitted that his draft of the State of the Union speech had been inadvertently chewed to bits by First Dog Bo, who apparently had been "hungry for some news about the nation."

David Axelrod, Senior Advisor to the President, shrugged off the incident but did hint that it revealed a disconcerting pattern of behavior. "First my tie, now the State of the Union. What will that pooch chow down next? New Jersey?"

First Dog Bo did not return repeated calls for comment. His whereabouts are currently unknown, though top White House sources tell us, "It's a safe bet he's in the doghouse as far as the President is concerned."

bo's tweets

 @ Bo Barks **State of the Union speech giving me bad case of indigestion. Funny, it tasted good at the time.**

about 5 hours ago from the web

 @ Bo Barks **Just finished tough questioning from the wags at Fox News about State of the Union speech. Took the Fifth and hightailed it to Rose Garden.**

about 2 hours ago from the web

 @ Bo Barks **Hiding out now in Situation Room. Secret Service after me for chewing up POTUS's speech. Who knew?**

3 minutes ago from the web

My every woof is scrutinized.

Every bone I munch is
written up in the press.

I'm a prisoner of
my own celebrity.

Ah, the price of fame...

NO AUTOGRAPHS!

NO PHOTO OPS!

I'VE GOT A DATE WITH A HYDRANT WITH MY NAME ON IT!

What's in a name?

Solving the mystery of why my human family chose the name "Bo."

Was I named for:

(hint, it may be more than one answer!)

A. Bo, the cat who belonged to cousins of Malia and Sasha?

B. The great jazz guitarist Bo Diddley?

C. First Lady Michelle's dad, who was nicknamed Diddley (after Bo Diddley)?

D. Bo Peep?

If you guessed B. and C., you're right.
If you guessed D., I don't want to hear a peep out of you!

BO TRIVIA: Other names that were in the running: "Frank" and "Moose."
(Moose? Do I look like Bullwinkle to you?!)

BO MAKES A SPLASH!

"He doesn't know how to swim," says Sasha after welcoming Bo to the family

The Washington Inside Scooper has learned that First Pooch Bo is being given secret swimming lessons. According to dog experts, Portuguese Water Dogs need to be taught how to swim, unlike other breeds who are instinctively adept at water sports. In an exclusive interview Bo reports, "I learned in no time. I'm great at the dog paddle. Just call me the next Michael Phelps!"

While the President met with leaders of the G-8, I had my own summit of the K-9!

Tea for two?
An audience with the Queen Pup?

Mamma Mia! Get a look at the dude without the fig leaf.

I didn't know this was a PG-13 museum!

Friends, Romans, countrymen, lend me your kibbles and treats!

STONEHENGE, ENGLAND

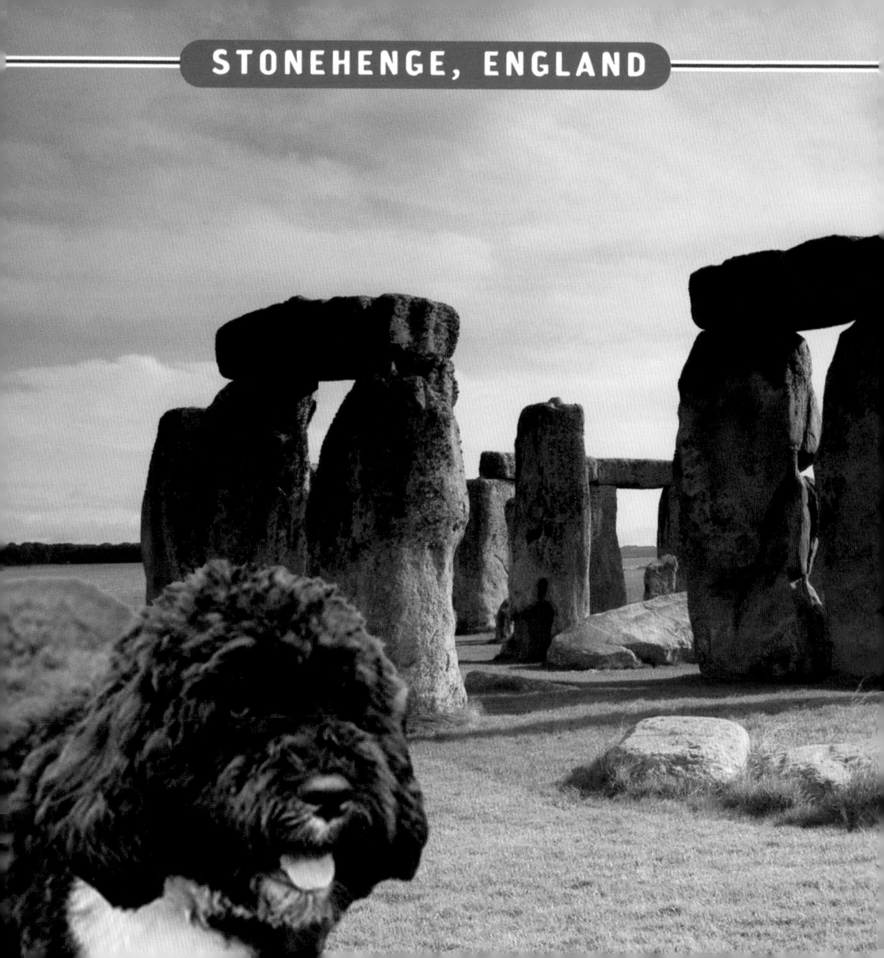

★★★
**Power jogging
with
POTUS**

"He's getting to the point where he can be naughty, like you walk in the room and it's like, 'Where'd you get that sock?'"

—FLOTUS MICHELLE

"If you want a friend
in Washington,
get a dog."

—PRESIDENT HARRY TRUMAN

"I have to say, Bo is the best puppy in the whole wide world."

—FIRST LADY MICHELLE

"Apparently, Portuguese Water Dogs like tomatoes. Michelle's garden is in danger."

—PRESIDENT BARACK OBAMA

Bo's Secret Fantasies...

One small step for dog, one giant leap for dogkind.

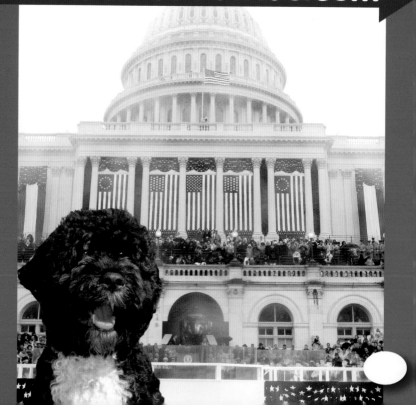

Bo's Secret Fantasies...

Ask not what your canine can do for you—ask what you can do for your canine.

Bo's Secret Fantasies...

This way to
your office,
Mr. President...

There's no place like home!